To

From

Date

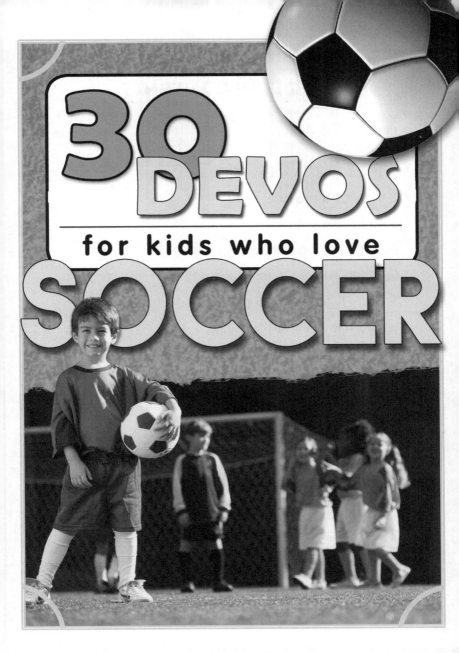

30 DEVOS

for kids who love

SOCCER

TABLE OF CONTENTS

Introduction

A MESSAGE FOR PARENTS

If your child's bookshelf is already spilling over with a happy assortment of good books for kids, congratulations—that means you're a thoughtful parent who understands the importance of reading to your child.

If your youngster plays soccer, this book is an important addition to his or her library. It is intended to be read by Christian parents to their young children. The text contains 30 brief devotionals, one for each day of the month. Each chapter consists of a Bible verse, a brief story, kid-friendly quotations, facts about soccer, tips for kids, and a prayer. Every devotional reading teaches a little about soccer and a lot about life.

For the next 30 days, take the time to read one chapter each night to your child, and then spend a few moments talking about the chapter's meaning. By the end of the month, you will have had 30 different opportunities to share God's wisdom with your son or daughter, and that's good . . . very good.

If you have been touched by God's love and His grace, then you know the joy that He has brought into your own life. Now it's your turn to share His message with the boy or girl whom He has entrusted to your care. Happy reading! And may God richly bless you and your family now and forever.

CHAPTER 1

If You're a Christian, Play Like One

*For I have given you an example
that you also should do
just as I have done for you.*

John 13:15 Holman CSB

TODAY'S BIG IDEA!

Since you're a Christian, you should behave like one all the time (including when you're on the soccer field).

What does the Bible say about being a good sport? Plenty! God's Word teaches us that we should treat other people like we'd want to be treated if we were in their shoes. And that means that we should be courteous and kind, on the field or off.

Where does kindness start? It starts in our hearts and works its way out from there. Jesus taught us that a pure heart is a wonderful blessing. It's up to each of us to fill our hearts with love for God, love for Jesus, and love for all people. When we do, we are blessed.

Do you want to be the best person you can be? Then invite the love of Christ into your heart and share His love with your family, with your friends, with your teammates, and with your opponents. And remember that lasting love always comes from a pure heart . . . like yours!

Kindness in this world will do
much to help others, not only
to come into the light, but also
to grow in grace day by day.

—

Fanny Crosby

When you launch an act of kindness
out into the crosswinds of life,
it will blow kindness back to you.

—

Dennis Swanberg

Be so preoccupied with good will
that you haven't room for ill will.

—

E. Stanley Jones

Make it a rule, and pray to God
to help you to keep it, never,
if possible, to lie down at night
without being able to say:
"I have made one human being at
least a little wiser, or a little happier,
or at least a little better this day."

—

Charles Kingsley

DID YOU KNOW?

⚽ People have played games that resembled soccer since the beginning of recorded history. But the first modern-day football association was founded in England in 1863. Thus Great Britain is generally credited with creating soccer as we know it today.

⚽ As far back as 3,000 years ago, the Chinese played a game that resembled soccer.

⚽ In almost every country except the United States, the game of soccer is called football.

ONE MORE THING TO REMEMBER

Showing good sportsmanship is more important than winning soccer games. God doesn't care whether you win or lose, but He does care how you treat other people. So behave yourself accordingly.

TODAY'S PRAYER

Dear Lord, give me the wisdom to be
a good sport, on the field and off.
Let me be humble when I win
and courteous when I lose,
today and every day. Amen

CHAPTER 2

Play by
the Golden Rule

*Therefore, whatever you want others
to do for you, do also the same for them—
this is the Law and the Prophets.*

Matthew 7:12 Holman CSB

TODAY'S BIG IDEA!

Practice makes perfect. So make sure you
always practice the Golden Rule!

When you're playing soccer, it's important to know the rules. And when you're trying to live a good life, it's essential to know God's rules. Jesus told us that we should treat other people in the same way that we would want to be treated: that's the Golden Rule—and it's a rule that you should obey every day.

God wants you to treat other people with respect, kindness, courtesy, and love. When you do, you make your family, your friends, and your teammates happy . . . and you make your Father in heaven very proud.

So if you're wondering how to treat someone else, ask the person you see every time you look into the mirror. The answer you receive will tell you exactly what to do.

DID YOU KNOW?

 Englishman J.C. Thring, attempting to bring order to the game of soccer, invented the Laws of the Game—"The Simplest Game," as he called it in 1862. Twenty-two players (11 on each team) would attempt to maneuver a ball into a goal or try to keep it out. A year after Thring's Laws were published, the London Football Association was founded and formalized a set of seventeen rules that govern play.

ONE MORE THING TO REMEMBER

What's good for you is good for them, too. If you want others to treat you according to the Golden Rule, then you should be quick to treat them in the same way. In other words, always play by the rule: the Golden Rule.

TODAY'S PRAYER

Dear Lord, help me always do
my very best to treat others as
I wish to be treated.
The Golden Rule is Your rule, Father;
let me also make it mine.
Amen

CHAPTER 3

Enjoy the Game

Light shines on those who do right;
joy belongs to those who are honest.
Rejoice in the Lord, you who do right.
Praise his holy name.

Psalm 97:11-12 NCV

TODAY'S BIG IDEA!

God wants you to live joyfully. And while you're out there on the soccer field, you should play joyfully, too.

God wants you to have a happy, joyful life. But that doesn't mean that you'll be happy all the time. Sometimes, you won't feel like feeling happy, and when you don't, your attitude won't be very good.

When you're feeling a little tired or sad, here's something to remember: This day is a gift from God. And it's up to you to enjoy this day by trying to be cheerful, helpful, courteous, and well behaved. How can you do these things? A good place to start is by doing your best to think good thoughts.

Joy cannot be pursued. It comes from within. It is a state of being. It does not depend on circumstances, but triumphs over circumstances. It produces a gentleness of spirit and a magnetic personality.

—

Billy Graham

Joy is the serious business of heaven.

—

C. S. Lewis

**Joy comes not from what we have
but from what we are.**

—

C. H. Spurgeon

DID YOU KNOW?

Soccer is the most popular sport in the world. More people play the game, and more people watch soccer than any other team sport.

In 1950, when Brazil played Uruguay in the World Cup in Rio de Janeiro, almost 200,000 crowded into the Maracana Municipal Stadium, setting an all time attendance record.

Soccer tournaments are often large, with many teams participating. But the largest ever occurred in 1999 in Bangkok with 5,098 teams and over 35,000 players.

ONE MORE THING TO REMEMBER

Every day, God gives us cause to rejoice. The rest is up to us.

TODAY'S PRAYER

Dear Lord, help me to feel
Your joy—and help me to share
it—today, tomorrow, and every day.
Amen

CHAPTER 4

Don't Be Too Hard on Yourself

Give all your worries and cares to God, for he cares about what happens to you.

1 Peter 5:6 NLT

TODAY'S BIG IDEA!

On the soccer pitch, don't be too afraid of making a mistake. Just do your best and expect the best.

Do you make mistakes on the soccer field . . . and off the field, too? Of course you do . . . everybody does. When you make a mistake, you must try your best to learn from it so that you won't make the very same mistake again. And, if you have hurt someone—or if you have disobeyed God—you must ask for forgiveness.

Remember: mistakes are a part of life, but the biggest mistake you can make is to keep making the same mistake over and over and over again.

**Father, take our mistakes
and turn them into opportunities.**

—

Max Lucado

**God is able to take mistakes,
when they are committed to Him,
and make of them something
for our good and for His glory.**

—

Ruth Bell Graham

If you learn from a defeat,
you have not really lost.

—

Zig Ziglar

It's your choice: you can either
count your blessings or
recount your disappointments.

—

Jim Gallery

DID YOU KNOW?

🌑 The governing body of soccer is the Federation Internationale de Football Association (FIFA), located in Zurich, Switzerland. FIFA sponsors the World Cup.

🌑 The World Cup is the most important international soccer competition, with the great soccer-playing nations competing against one another. The World Cup has been awarded every four years since 1930, with the exception of 1942 and 1946 (in those years, games were cancelled due to World War II).

🌑 The World Cup finals have always included a European soccer team with the exception of 1930 and 1950.

ONE MORE THING TO REMEMBER

When you make a mistake, learn something
. . . and forgive someone: yourself. Remember, you don't have to be perfect to be wonderful.

TODAY'S PRAYER

Dear Lord, sometimes I make
mistakes. When I do, help me learn
something, help me forgive myself,
and help me become a smarter
person today than I was yesterday.
Amen

CHAPTER 5

When You're On the Soccer Field, Play with the Right Attitude

Keep your eyes focused on what is right, and look straight ahead to what is good.

Proverbs 4:25 NCV

TODAY'S BIG IDEA!

On the soccer field or off, your attitude is important. So guard your thoughts carefully . . . and try not to lose control.

What does the word "attitude" mean? "Attitude" means "the way that you think." And your attitude is important in the game of soccer and in the game of life. Your attitude can make you happy or sad, grumpy or glad, joyful or mad. Your attitude doesn't just control the way that you think; it also controls how you play the game. If you have a good attitude, you'll be a better player. But if you have a bad attitude, you're more likely to misbehave.

Have you spent any time thinking about the way that you think? Hopefully so! After all, a good attitude is better than a bad one . . . lots better.

You have more control over your attitude than you think. One way you can improve your attitude is by learning about Jesus and about His attitude toward life. When you do, you'll learn that it's always better to think good thoughts, and it's always better to do good things. Always!

Attitude is the mind's paintbrush; it can color any situation.

—

Barbara Johnson

A positive attitude will have positive results because attitudes are contagious.

—

Zig Ziglar

All things being equal, attitude wins.
All things not being equal,
attitude sometimes still wins.

—

John Maxwell

Developing a positive attitude means
working continually to find what is
uplifting and encouraging.

—

Barbara Johnson

DID YOU KNOW?

⚽ Most experts consider the Brazilian legend Pelé to be the greatest soccer player of all time. And the International Olympic Committee named Pelé the greatest athlete of the 20th century.

NOW HEAR THIS!

**Enthusiasm is everything.
It must be as taut and vibrating
as a guitar string.**

—

Pelé

ONE MORE THING TO REMEMBER

A good attitude leads to positive results; a bad attitude leads elsewhere.

TODAY'S PRAYER

Dear Lord, I pray for an attitude that pleases You. Even when I'm angry, unhappy, tired, or upset, I pray that I can remember what it means to be a good person and a good Christian.
Amen

CHAPTER 6

Learn to Control Your Anger

Those who control their anger have great understanding; those with a hasty temper will make mistakes.

Proverbs 14:29 NLT

TODAY'S BIG IDEA!

When things don't go your way, you may be tempted to become angry. Very angry. But if you're wise, you'll learn to control your anger before it controls you.

Sometimes, when you're playing soccer, you may get angry. Either you make a mistake or somebody else does, and you feel your temper starting to boil. When you become angry, you may say something or do something that you'll regret later. That's why you should learn to control your anger before it controls you.

Jesus does not intend that you strike out against other people, and He doesn't intend that your heart be troubled by anger. Your heart should instead be filled with love, just like Jesus' heart was . . . and is!

When you strike out in anger,
you may miss the other person,
but you will always hit yourself.

—

Jim Gallery

Anger is the noise of the soul;
the unseen irritant of the heart;
the relentless invader of silence.

—

Max Lucado

Bitterness and anger, usually over little things, create big troubles in homes, churches, and friendships.

—

Warren Wiersbe

Get rid of the poison of built-up anger.

—

Charles Swindoll

DID YOU KNOW?

⚽ In the year 2000, an Internet poll was taken to name the greatest soccer player of the 20th century. Diego Maradona, who first played for the Argentine national team at the tender age of 16, was named the people's player of the century. However many soccer experts (including the officials at FIFA) still consider Pelé to be the greatest player of all time.

NOW HEAR THIS!

God makes me play well.
That is why I always make the sign of the cross when I walk out onto the field.

—

Diego Maradona

ONE MORE THING TO REMEMBER

If you think you're about to explode in anger, don't! Instead of striking back at someone, it's better to slow down, catch your breath, consider your options, and walk away if you must.

TODAY'S PRAYER

Lord, when I become angry, help me to remember that You offer me peace. Let me turn to You for wisdom, for patience, and for the peace that only You can give.
Amen

CHAPTER 7

You Can Do It . . . If You Stick to It!

We say they are happy because they did not give up.

James 5:11 NCV

TODAY'S BIG IDEA!

If you want to be a champion, you can't give up at the first sign of trouble. So if at first you don't succeed, keep trying until you do.

n soccer and in life, the way you think determines the way you play. If you think you can do something, then you can probably do it. If you think you can't do something, then you probably won't do it.

So remember this: if you're having a little trouble getting something done, don't get mad, don't get frustrated, don't get discouraged, and don't give up. Just keep trying . . . and believe in yourself.

When you try hard—and keep trying hard—you can really do amazing things . . . but if you quit at the first sign of trouble, you'll miss out. So here's a good rule to follow: when you have something that you want to finish, finish it . . . and finish it sooner rather than later.

Don't quit. For if you do, you may miss the answer to your prayers.

—

Max Lucado

Keep advancing; do not stop, do not turn back, do not turn from the straight road.

—

St. Augustine

The hardest part of a journey
is neither the start nor the finish,
but the middle mile.

—

Vance Havner

When you fall and skin your knees
and skin your heart,
He'll pick you up.

—

Charles Stanley

DID YOU KNOW?

⚽ In soccer, a goalie wears a different colored shirt than other members of his team. This tradition was begun in the early 1900s.

⚽ Lev Yashin, who played for Russia from 1951-1970, is considered by many to be the greatest goaltender of all time. In 1963, he was the first Russian to win the European Footballer of the Year award, and he remains the only goaltender to have won the honor.

NOW HEAR THIS!

Failure happens all the time. It happens every day in practice. What makes you better is how you react to it.

—

Mia Hamm

ONE MORE THING TO REMEMBER

If things don't work out at first, don't quit. If you don't keep trying, you'll never know how good you can be.

TODAY'S PRAYER

Dear Lord, sometimes I feel like giving up. When I feel that way, help me do the right thing . . . and help me finish the work You want me to do.
Amen

CHAPTER 8

Don't Be a Chronic Complainer!

Be hospitable to one another without complaining.
1 Peter 4:9 Holman CSB

TODAY'S BIG IDEA!

On the soccer field, lots of players (and fans) find reasons to complain. But you should never become a chronic complainer. Instead of worrying about bad calls, think carefully about your own play.

When things don't go your way on the soccer field, are you tempted to complain? Or pout? Or whine? If so, it's time to change the way you think and the way you behave.

Some kids think that whining is a good way to get the things they want (but hopefully you're wiser than that). In truth, whining doesn't work for long. So if your parents or your coach ask you to do something, don't complain about it. And if there's something you want, don't whine and complain until you get it.

Remember: whining won't make you happy . . . and it won't make anybody else happy, either.

Just as courage is faith in good, so discouragement is faith in evil, and, while courage opens the door to good, discouragement opens it to evil.

—

Hannah Whitall Smith

Jesus wept, but he never complained.

—

C. H. Spurgeon

When you're on the verge of
throwing a pity party thanks to
your despairing thoughts,
go back to the Word of God.

—

Charles Swindoll

Shine—don't whine.

—

Anonymous

DID YOU KNOW?

🌑 Soccer is tough enough without wardrobe problems. In the 1938 World Cup semifinal, while taking a penalty shot, an Italian player named Guiseppe Meazza was surprised when his shorts fell down. He calmly reached down, held onto his shorts, and scored the goal.

🌑 Many soccer players use shinguards to protect their legs. Shinguards were first introduced in 1874 by Sam Widdowson of Nottingham Forest.

ONE MORE THING TO REMEMBER

Constant complaining is a bad habit—make sure it's not your bad habit!

TODAY'S PRAYER

Lord, I know that the choice
is mine—I can either count my
blessings or recount my
disappointments. Today, help me
to focus my thoughts upon
my blessings, my gifts,
and my opportunities.
Amen

CHAPTER 9

Learn to Control Yourself

So prepare your minds for service and have self-control. All your hope should be for the gift of grace that will be yours when Jesus Christ is shown to you.

1 Peter 1:13 NCV

TODAY'S BIG IDEA!

When you play sports, you should try to learn self-discipline and self-control. The sooner you learn how to control yourself, the better.

Are you learning how to control your-self on the soccer field and off? If the answer to that question is yes, then you deserve a big cheer because God wants all His children (including you) to be-have themselves.

Sometimes, it's hard to be a person who is well-behaved, especially if you and your teammates become wrapped up in the outcome of a game. But if your teammates misbehave, don't imitate them. Instead, listen to your conscience, and do the right thing . . . RIGHT NOW!

Your thoughts are the determining
factor as to whose mold you are
conformed to. Control your
thoughts and you control
the direction of your life.

—

Charles Stanley

If one examines the secret behind
a championship football team,
a magnificent orchestra, or
a successful business, the principal
ingredient is invariably discipline.

—

James Dobson

**True will power and courage
are not only on the battlefield,
but also in those everyday victories.**

—

D. L. Moody

DID YOU KNOW?

🌐 Many fans and experts believe that America's Mia Hamm is the greatest woman soccer player in history. During her amazing career, she has earned four NCAA titles (at North Carolina), an Olympic gold medal, two World Cup championships, and five U.S. Female Player of the Year awards. Wow!

NOW HEAR THIS!

Success is usually the result of
the old-fashioned, basic concepts
like hard work, determination,
good planning, and perseverance.

—

Mia Hamm

ONE MORE THING TO REMEMBER

Sometimes, the best way to control yourself is to slow yourself down. Then, you can think about the things you're about to do before you do them.

TODAY'S PRAYER

Dear Lord, the Bible teaches me that it's good to be able to control myself. Today, I will slow myself down and think about things before I do things.
Amen

CHAPTER 10

Keep Learning

Remember what you are taught.
And listen carefully to words of knowledge.
Proverbs 23:12 ICB

TODAY'S BIG IDEA!

Even if you've already learned a lot about soccer, you've still got a lot to learn. And even if you've already learned a lot about life, you've still got a lot to learn. So keep learning.

Do you know all there is to know about soccer . . . or about anything else, for that matter? Of course you don't! Even if you've already learned a lot, there's still more to learn—on the soccer field and off.

When it comes to learning life's lessons, you can either do things the easy way or the hard way. The easy way can be summed up as follows: when you're supposed to learn something, you learn it the first time! Unfortunately, lots of people (but hopefully not you) learn much more slowly than that.

So today and every day, do yourself a big favor by learning your lessons sooner rather than later. Because the sooner you do, the sooner you can move on to the next lesson and the next and the next.

Knowledge is power.

—

Francis Bacon

The more wisdom enters our hearts,
the more we will be able to trust our
hearts in difficult situations.

—

John Eldredge

**The doorstep to the temple
of wisdom is a knowledge
of our own ignorance.**

—

C. H. Spurgeon

**It's the things you learn after you
know it all that really count.**

—

Vance Havner

DID YOU KNOW?

⚽ Franz Beckenbauer of Germany is the only player in history to have won the World Cup as both a player (1974) and a manager (1990).

⚽ The first African player to gain world-wide recognition was Eusebio. For most of his career, he played for Portugal. Eusebio was called the "European Pelé" and is still considered the greatest Portuguese player of all time.

NOW HEAR THIS!

I had soccer under my skin.

—

Eusebio

ONE MORE THING TO REMEMBER

If you think you know it all, think again!

TODAY'S PRAYER

Dear Lord, I have lots to learn.
Help me to watch, to listen, to think,
and to learn every day of my life.
Amen

CHAPTER 11

Listen to Your Coach

*If you listen to constructive criticism,
you will be at home among the wise.*

Proverbs 15:31 NLT

TODAY'S BIG IDEA!

Your coach has lots to teach you, but you can't learn much while you're talking. So when your coach is talking, make sure that you're listening.

Directions, directions, and more directions. Whether you're playing soccer or going to school, it seems like somebody is always giving you directions: telling you where to go, how to behave, and what to do next. But sometimes all these directions can be confusing! How can you understand everything that everybody tells you? The answer, of course, is that you must pay careful attention to those directions . . . and that means listening.

To become a careful listener, here are some things you must do: 1. Don't talk when you're supposed to be listening (your ears work best when your mouth is closed); 2. Watch the person who's giving the directions (when your eyes and ears work together, it's easier to understand things); 3. If you don't understand something, ask a question (it's better to ask now than to make a mistake later).

God gave us two ears
and one mouth for a good reason:
so we could listen
twice as much as we talk.

—

Old Saying

Wise people listen
to wise instruction.

—

Warren Wiersbe

It takes a wise person to give good advice, but an even wiser person to take it.

—

Marie T. Freeman

Part of good communication is listening with the eyes as well as with the ears.

—

Josh McDowell

DID YOU KNOW?

 Who's the greatest English soccer player of all time? Today, we think of Beckham, but many experts give that honor to Bobby Charlton who enjoyed a 17-season career with Manchester United, the team that became the first English club to win the European Cup (1968). Charlton also played a crucial role in England's only World Cup victory (1966).

ONE MORE THING TO REMEMBER

When you listen to the things your coach has to say, it shows that you care. Listening carefully is not just the courteous thing to do; it's also the respectful thing to do.

TODAY'S PRAYER

Dear Lord, make me a good listener, especially when I'm listening to people who have much to teach me. Amen

CHAPTER 12

Watch What You Say!

Pleasant words are like a honeycomb.
They make a person happy and healthy.
Proverbs 16:24 ICB

TODAY'S BIG IDEA!

Do you like for people to say nice words to you? Yes you do! And that's exactly how other people feel, too. That's why it's important to say things that make people feel better, not worse.

Are you careful about the things you say, on the field or off? If your answer is yes, that's good because the words you speak are important. If you speak kind words, you make other people feel better. And that's exactly what God wants you to do!

How hard is it to say a kind word? Not very! Yet sometimes we're so busy that we forget to say the very things that might make other people feel better.

Kind words help; cruel words hurt. It's as simple as that. And, when we say the right thing at the right time, we give a gift that can change somebody's game, somebody's day, or somebody's life.

**Attitude and the spirit in which
we communicate are as important
as the words we say.**

—

Charles Stanley

**Change the heart,
and you change the speech.**

—

Warren Wiersbe

Fill the heart with the love of Christ
so that only truth and purity
can come out of the mouth.

—

Warren Wiersbe

When you talk, choose the very same
words that you would use
if Jesus were looking over
your shoulder. Because He is.

—

Marie T. Freeman

DID YOU KNOW?

 Sir Stanley Matthews was a legendary British player who was considered in his day to be the finest dribbler ever produced by England. Although Matthews did score on occasion, his greatest value was as a passer. He enjoyed an extraordinary 34-year playing career in the first division soccer (Matthews was still playing first division at age 50) and was knighted by his country in 1965, an unprecedented honor at the time.

ONE MORE THING TO REMEMBER

If you can't think of something nice to say, keep thinking (and keep quiet) until you can think of the right words. It's better to say nothing than to hurt someone's feelings.

TODAY'S PRAYER

Dear Lord, You hear every word that
I say. Help me remember to
speak words that are honest,
kind, and helpful.
Amen

CHAPTER 13

Try Your Hardest!

Whatever you do, do it enthusiastically, as something done for the Lord and not for men.

Colossians 3:23 Holman CSB

TODAY'S BIG IDEA!

Wherever you happen to be—whether you're on the soccer field or at school, or anywhere in between—try to do your best. When you work hard, and keep working hard, you'll earn big rewards.

Whether you're practicing or playing in a game, you know that you should give your best effort. But sometimes, especially when you get tired, you'll be tempted to slow down or give up altogether. Don't do it! Keep trying, even when you're tired or discouraged, or both.

Face facts: Life's biggest rewards aren't likely to fall into your lap. Your greatest accomplishments will probably require plenty of effort, which is perfectly fine with God. After all, He knows that you're up to it, and He has big plans for you. God will do His part to fulfill those plans, and the rest, of course, is up to you.

**Success or failure can be
pretty well predicted by the degree
to which the heart is fully in it.**

—

John Eldredge

**We must trust as if it
all depended on God and
work as if it all depended on us.**

—

C. H. Spurgeon

Few things fire up a person's commitment like dedication to excellence.

—

John Maxwell

You can't climb the ladder of life with your hands in your pockets.

—

Barbara Johnson

DID YOU KNOW?

🌐 In the early 1900s, Brazilians fell in love with the game of soccer. As early as 1919, clubs were founded in the Amazon basin. The unparalleled success of its national teams in international competition has only increased the country's legendary status as the world's greatest soccer-playing nation.

🌐 All great Brazilian soccer players go by one name. That's why **Marta Vieira da Silva**, perhaps the greatest woman player in the world, is known, simply, as **Marta**. In 2006, at the age of 20, she became the youngest woman ever to win the **FIFA World Player of the Year**.

ONE MORE THING TO REMEMBER

Sooner or later, practice has a way of pay-
ing off (and it's usually sooner).

TODAY'S PRAYER

Dear Lord, when I'm on
the soccer field, or anywhere else,
let me try my hardest. Let me do my
best and leave the rest to You.
Amen

CHAPTER 14

Always Be Honest

*Tell each other the truth because
we all belong to each other . . . .*
Ephesians 4:25 ICB

TODAY'S BIG IDEA!

No matter where you happen to be, be honest. And play fair.

Whether you're playing sports or working in the classroom, or anywhere else for that matter, it's important to be honest. When you tell the truth, you'll feel better about yourself, and other people will feel better about you, too. But that's not all. When you tell the truth, God knows—and He will reward you for your honesty.

Telling the truth is hard sometimes. But it's better to be honest, even when it's hard. So remember this: telling the truth is always the right thing to do . . . always.

God doesn't expect you to be
perfect, but he does insist
on complete honesty.

—

Rick Warren

Lying covers a multitude of sins—
temporarily.

—

D. L. Moody

You cannot glorify Christ
and practice dishonesty
at the same time.

Warren Wiersbe

Those who walk in truth walk
in liberty.

Beth Moore

DID YOU KNOW?

⚽ Soccer balls come in three different sizes: 3, 4, and 5 (the size is printed on the ball). Quality balls usually bear the words "official size & weight" or "FIFA Approved." But even if a ball is the official size and weight, it's important to remember that some balls are heavier and harder than other balls. And if you're smart, you won't use a ball that's too heavy or too hard.

⚽ A rugby player named J. Brodie is credited with the idea of using goal nets. He patented his brainchild in 1890, and in a few years, all clubs were using nets.

ONE MORE THING TO REMEMBER

Honesty is the best policy. Make sure that it's your policy, even when telling the truth makes you feel a little uncomfortable.

TODAY'S PRAYER

Dear Lord, I know that it's important to be an honest person. Since I want other people to be truthful with me, let me be truthful with them, today and every day.
Amen

CHAPTER 15

Be a Good Example

You are the light that gives light to the world . . . Live so that they will see the good things you do. Live so that they will praise your Father in heaven.

Matthew 5:14, 16 ICB

TODAY'S BIG IDEA!

Whether you're on the soccer field or off it, your friends are watching. So be the kind of example that God wants you to be—be a good example.

When you're playing soccer—or doing anything else—what kind of example are you? Are you the kind of person who shows other kids what it means to be a Christian? Are you a good sport and a team player? And do you always try your hardest? Hopefully so!!!

When you do the right thing, you're bound to be a good example to other kids. And that's good because God needs people like you who are willing to stand up and be counted for Him.

**The best evidence of our having
the truth is our walking in the truth.**

—

Matthew Henry

**I don't care what a person says
he believes with his lips.
I want to know what he says
with his life and his actions.**

—

Sam Jones

Never support an experience
which does not have God as its
source and faith in God as its result.

—

Oswald Chambers

More depends on my walk
than my talk.

—

D. L. Moody

NOW HEAR THIS!

So celebrate what you've accomplished, but raise the bar a little higher each time you succeed.

—

Mia Hamm

Keep training, keep looking forward, and don't look back.

—

Renaldo

True champions aren't always the ones that win, but those with the most courage and guts.

—

Mia Hamm

ONE MORE THING TO REMEMBER

God wants you to be a good example to your family, to your friends, and to the world.

TODAY'S PRAYER

Lord, make me a good example
to my family and friends.
Let the things that I say and do show
everybody what it means to be a
good person and a good Christian.
Amen

CHAPTER 16

On the Field or Off, Be Thankful

I will give You thanks with all my heart.
Psalm 138:1 Holman CSB

TODAY'S BIG IDEA!

It's important to be thankful for all your opportunities, including the opportunity to enjoy sports like soccer.

If you sat down and began counting your blessings, how long would it take? A very, very long time! Your blessings include your life, your family, your teammates, your talents, your coaches, and your possessions, for starters. But, your greatest blessing—a gift that is yours for the asking—is God's gift of eternal life through Christ Jesus.

You can never count up every single blessing that God has given you, but it doesn't hurt to try . . . so get ready, get set, go—start counting your blessings RIGHT NOW!

The joy of the Holy Spirit is experienced by giving thanks in all situations.

—

Bill Bright

Thanksgiving or complaining—these words express two contrastive attitudes of the souls of God's children in regard to His dealings with them. The soul that gives thanks can find comfort in everything; the soul that complains can find comfort in nothing.

—

Hannah Whitall Smith

**Thanksgiving is good
but Thanksliving is better.**

—

Jim Gallery

**It is always possible to be thankful
for what is given rather than
to complain about what is not given.
One or the other becomes
a habit of life.**

—

Elisabeth Elliot

DID YOU KNOW?

When a player is shown a yellow card by the referee, it means that player has committed a serious foul and may be ejected from the game in the event of a second rules violation.

When a player is shown a red card by the referee, that player is automatically ejected from the game and cannot be replaced.

Some soccer players simply don't behave themselves. During a match in Paraguay in 1993, 20 red cards were shown!

ONE MORE THING TO REMEMBER

Two magic words: Thank you! Your parents and coaches will never become tired of hearing those two little words, and neither will God. And while you're at it, try three more: "I love you!"

TODAY'S PRAYER

Dear Lord, I am a very lucky person,
and I thank You for my blessings.
Help me to be a good person,
and help me use my talents for
Your glory . . . and for Your Son.
Amen

CHAPTER 17

Patience Pays

Always be humble and gentle.
Be patient and accept each other
with love.

Ephesians 4:2 ICB

TODAY'S BIG IDEA!

Haven't scored a goal yet? Be patient! The
Bible says that patience pays, and the Bible
is always right.

The dictionary defines the word "patience" as "the ability to be calm, tolerant, and understanding." Here's what that means: the word "calm" means being in control of your emotions (not letting your emotions control you). The word "tolerant" means being kind and considerate to people who are different from you. And, the word "understanding" means being able to put yourself in another person's shoes.

If you can be calm, tolerant, and understanding—both on the soccer field and off—you will be the kind of person whose good deeds are a blessing to your family, to your friends, to your coaches, and to your teammates. And that's exactly the kind of person that God wants you to be.

The next time you're disappointed,
don't panic. Don't give up.
Just be patient and let God remind
you he's still in control.

—

Max Lucado

Patience is the companion
of wisdom.

—

St. Augustine

Our Lord worked with people
as they were, and He was patient—
not tolerant of sin,
but compassionate.

—

Vance Havner

God gave everyone patience—
wise people use it.

—

Anonymous

DID YOU KNOW?

🌐 Americans usually think of the word "dribbling" as a basketball term, but dribbling also happens on the soccer field. When a soccer player controls the ball with his or her foot and moves the ball around the soccer field, that's dribbling, too!

🌐 In what was called one of the biggest upsets in the history of soccer, the USA defeated England 1-0 in the opening round of the 1950 World Cup held in Brazil. Joe Baetjen scored the only goal of the game.

🌐 Over 90,000 fans crowded into the Rose Bowl in 1999 to cheer the US Women's National Team to a Women's World Cup. The Americans defeated China in overtime, 5-4.

ONE MORE THING TO REMEMBER

If you think you're about to say or do something you'll regret later, slow down and take a deep breath, or two deep breaths or ten or . . . well you get the idea.

TODAY'S PRAYER

Dear Lord, sometimes it's hard to be patient, and that's exactly when I should try my hardest to be patient. Help me to obey You by being a patient, loving person . . . even when it's hard.
Amen

CHAPTER 18

Blaming Others . . .

An angry person causes trouble.

Proverbs 29:22 NCV

TODAY'S BIG IDEA!

If you run into problems on the soccer pitch, you may be tempted to blame your teammates (or the referee). But don't start spreading the blame—the blame game only leads to trouble.

When something goes wrong, do you look for somebody to blame? And do you try to blame other people even if you're the one who made the mistake? Hopefully not!

In the game of soccer (and in the game of life) it's tempting to blame everybody (except yourself!). But the blame game is a game with no winners. So if things aren't going your way, don't look for somebody to blame; look for some way to make things better. Because playing the blame game doesn't work, and while you're playing it, neither do you.

You'll never win the blame game,
so why even bother to play?

—

Marie T. Freeman

There comes a time when we simply
have to face the challenges in our
lives and stop backing down.

—

John Eldredge

**The main thing is this:
we should never blame anyone
or anything for our defeats.**

—

A. W. Tozer

DID YOU KNOW?

 Kyle Rote, Jr., the son of a football star, was one of the first stars of American soccer. As a rookie in 1973, he was the first American to win the North American Soccer League scoring title (with 10 goals and 10 assists).

ONE MORE THING TO REMEMBER

Don't try to blame other people for the mistakes you make. When you point your finger at someone else, the rest of your fingers are pointing back at you!

TODAY'S PRAYER

Dear Lord, when I make a mistake, I want to admit it. Help me to not blame others for the mistakes that I make. And when I make a mistake, help me to learn from it.
Amen

CHAPTER 19

Respect the Rules!

It's quite simple: Do what is fair and just to your neighbor, be compassionate and loyal in your love, and don't take yourself too seriously—take God seriously.

Micah 6:8 MSG

TODAY'S BIG IDEA!

God has rules (which you should always try to obey) and the game of soccer has rules, too. You're never too young to play by the rules.

When you're playing sports, do you try to obey the rules? And do you try to obey God's rules all day long, every day? Hopefully so!

An attitude of obedience starts in your heart and works its way out from there. That's why it's important to listen to your heart when it tells you how to behave. When you do, you'll be happier, healthier, smarter, and safer.

So don't forget to listen to your parents and your coaches. And don't forget to listen to your conscience. When you listen carefully, you'll obey the rules . . . and you'll make everybody glad, including yourself!

When the law of God is
written on our hearts,
our duty will be our delight.

—

Matthew Henry

Although God causes all things
to work together for good for His
children, He still holds us
accountable for our behavior.

—

Kay Arthur

Obedience is the outward
expression of your love of God.

Henry Blackaby

There may be no trumpet sound or
loud applause when we make
a right decision, just a calm sense
of resolution and peace.

Gloria Gaither

DID YOU KNOW?

🌑 The Romans played a tough kind of soccer, a game played by hundreds of soldiers. In the early Olympic games played in Rome, fully two thirds of the players were injured.

🌑 England is credited with developing the form of soccer that is played today. But soccer was not always looked upon with favor in England. King Edward (1303-1327) imprisoned anyone caught playing soccer. He thought soccer caused "great noise" and "many evils." Queen Elizabeth I had soccer players jailed for a week with "follow-up church penance."

ONE MORE THING TO REMEMBER

Remember: Rules aren't made to be broken. Rules are made to be obeyed!

TODAY'S PRAYER

Dear Lord, when I play by
Your rules, You bless my life.
But, when I disobey Your rules,
I suffer the consequences.
Help me play by the rules
today and every day.
Amen

CHAPTER 20

Listen to Your Conscience

They show that in their hearts they know what is right and wrong.

Romans 2:15 ICB

TODAY'S BIG IDEA!

Whether you're on the soccer field or someplace else, listen to your conscience. If you listen to your conscience, you'll do the right thing.

G od gave you something called a conscience: some people describe it as a little voice, but really, it's a feeling—it's a feeling that tells you whether something is right or wrong. Your conscience will usually tell you what to do and when to do it. Pay attention to that feeling, and trust it.

If you slow down and listen to your conscience, you'll usually stay out of trouble. And if you listen to your conscience, it won't be so hard to control your own behavior. Why? Because most of the time, your conscience already knows right from wrong. So don't be in such a hurry to do things. Instead of "jumping right in," listen to your conscience. In the end, you'll be very glad you did.

**Your conscience is
your alarm system.
It's your protection.**

—

Charles Stanley

**It is neither safe nor prudent
to do anything against
one's conscience.**

—

Martin Luther

Guilt is a healthy regret for telling God one thing and doing another.

—

Max Lucado

One's conscience can only be satisfied when God is satisfied.

—

C. H. Spurgeon

DID YOU KNOW?

⚽ The average number of goals scored in a typical soccer match is relatively low, about 2.5 per game.

⚽ A soccer player runs an average of 7 to 10 miles during the course of a game, 2,000 yards of which is all-out sprinting.

ONE MORE THING TO REMEMBER

If you're not sure it's the right thing to do . . . listen to your conscience and talk to your parents (or to your coach).

TODAY'S PRAYER

Dear Lord, You have given me
a conscience that tells me what
is right and what is wrong.
I will listen to that quiet voice
so I can do the right thing
today and every day.
Amen

CHAPTER 21

Respect Everybody (Including the Players on the Other Team!)

Show respect for all people.
Love the brothers and sisters
of God's family.
1 Peter 2:17 ICB

TODAY'S BIG IDEA!

You should treat all players with respect. That means you should be kind to your teammates and to the players on the other team.

Do you try to have a respectful attitude toward your teammates? And do you show respect for the players on the other team, too? Hopefully, you can answer these questions with a great, big YES!

The Bible teaches us to treat all people with respect. And showing respect for others is habit-forming: the more you do it, the easier it becomes. So start practicing right now. Say lots of kind words and do lots of kind things, because when it comes to kindness and respect, practice makes perfect.

God shows unbridled delight
when He sees people acting
in ways that honor Him,
when He sees tender love shared
among His people.

—

Bill Hybels

Courtesy is contagious.

—

Marie T. Freeman

When you received Jesus Christ
as your personal Lord and Savior,
you began a relationship
not only with Him but also
with all other Christians.

—

Billy Graham

The Lord Jesus Christ enables us
all to be family.

—

Dennis Swanberg

DID YOU KNOW?

⚽ On the southeastern outskirts of Mexico City, on an open tract of land, stands the giant Aztec Stadium. It holds 115,000 people. But the Morumbi Stadium in São Paulo, Brazil was, for a while, even bigger. At one time, it held 140,000 fans.

⚽ One of the world's most revered soccer stadiums is Wembley Stadium in London. Wembley is, in a sense, a shrine to the game itself—the equivalent of baseball's Yankee Stadium. Oddly enough, both Wembley Stadium and Yankee Stadium were built in 1923.

ONE MORE THING TO REMEMBER

When it comes to the game of soccer, you can be sure that your coach knows more than you do . . . so listen and learn.

TODAY'S PRAYER

Dear Lord, I will try to show respect
to everybody, starting with
my family and my friends.
And, I will do my best to share
the love that I feel in my heart
for them . . . and for You!
Amen

CHAPTER 22

When Other Players Aren't Nice

Whoever forgives someone's sin makes a friend . . . .

Proverbs 17:9 NCV

TODAY'S BIG IDEA!

You may play against kids who don't behave themselves. If so, you should forgive them as quickly as possible and move on . . . as quickly as possible.

The Bible tells us this: When other people do things that are wrong, we should forgive them. God's Word also tells us that when we're willing to forgive others, God is quick to forgive us for the mistakes we make.

Has somebody done something—either on the soccer field or someplace else—that has made you angry? If so, you should make up your mind to forgive the person who has hurt your feelings. And remember: God wants you to hurry up and forgive others, just like God is always in a hurry to forgive you.

A keen sense of humor helps us to overlook the unbecoming, understand the unconventional, tolerate the unpleasant, overcome the unexpected, and outlast the unbearable.

—

Billy Graham

Only the truly forgiven are truly forgiving.

—

C. S. Lewis

Our relationships with other people
are of primary importance to God.
Because God is love, He cannot
tolerate any unforgiveness
or hardness in us toward
any individual.

—

Catherine Marshall

Forgiveness is not an emotion.
Forgiveness is an act of the will,
and the will can function regardless
of the temperature of the heart.

—

Corrie ten Boom

DID YOU KNOW?

⚽ France's Just Fontaine is still the record-holder for most goals in the final round of World Cup competition with 13 goals scored during six games in the 1958 Cup. While leading his country to a third-place finish, he saved the best for last, netting four goals in the consolation-game win over West Germany.

NOW HEAR THIS!

There are always new,
grander challenges to confront,
and a true winner
will embrace each one.

—

Mia Hamm

ONE MORE THING TO REMEMBER

If you're having trouble forgiving someone else . . . think about how many times other people have forgiven you!

TODAY'S PRAYER

Dear Lord, when somebody hurts my feelings, let me be patient and kind. And when a friend does something wrong, help me do the right thing by offering my forgiveness sooner rather than later!
Amen

CHAPTER 23

Be a Team Player

You're blessed when you can show people how to cooperate instead of compete or fight.

Matthew 5:9 MSG

TODAY'S BIG IDEA!

Teamwork works. Selfishness doesn't.

As you play the game of soccer (or the game of life), you need teammates. And when you think about it, being a good teammate is simple: It just means that you're willing to help the other kids on your team become better players.

Helping other people can be fun! When you help others, you feel better about yourself—and you know that God approves of what you're doing. And when you cooperate with your family, with your friends, and with your teammates, you'll soon discover that it's more fun when everybody works together. So do everybody (including yourself) a big favor: Learn better ways to share and better ways to cooperate. When you do, everybody wins.

Enthusiasm, like the flu,
is contagious—
we get it from one another.

—

Barbara Johnson

Encouraging others means
helping people, looking for
the best in them, and trying to
bring out their positive qualities.

—

John Maxwell

How many people stop
because so few say, "Go!"

—

Charles Swindoll

A lot of people have gone further
than they thought they could
because someone else
thought they could.

—

Zig Ziglar

DID YOU KNOW?

🔲 A soccer field is not more than 120 yards long, not less than 110. Its width: 80 yards maximum, 70 minimum.

NOW HEAR THIS!

I am a member of a team,
and I rely on the team.
I defer to it and sacrifice for it
because the team, not the individual,
is the ultimate champion.

—

Mia Hamm

ONE MORE THING TO REMEMBER

You can do things to make your teammates better players, and they can do things to make you a better player, too. So don't be a selfish player. Think of the team first, not yourself.

TODAY'S PRAYER

Dear Lord, help me be a team player
today and every day. Let me look
for the best in my teammates,
and help me be more interested in
my team's success than I am
in my own success.
Amen

The happiest people in the world
are not those who have no problems,
but the people who have learned
to live with things that
are less than perfect.

—

James Dobson

What makes a Christian a Christian is
not perfection but forgiveness.

—

Max Lucado

God doesn't expect you to live
a mistake-free life—
and neither should you.

—

Criswell Freeman

We are all on our way somewhere.
We'll get there if we just keep going.

—

Barbara Johnson

DID YOU KNOW?

⚽ The penalty box is the large area in front of the goal in which the goalkeeper can touch the ball with their hands.

⚽ All players on the field except the goalkeeper are called (not surprisingly) "field players." However, when the goalkeeper moves outside the penalty box, he or she loses special privileges and becomes a field player, too (until returning to the penalty box).

NOW HEAR THIS!

Self-confidence is the hallmark of a champion . . . any champion.

—

Grantland Rice

ONE MORE THING TO REMEMBER

If you hear a little voice inside your head telling you that you'll never be good enough . . . don't pay attention to that little voice. God loves you . . . and if you're good enough for God, you're good enough.

TODAY'S PRAYER

Dear Lord, help me remember
that I don't have to be perfect
to be wonderful.
Amen

CHAPTER 25

Don't Be a Chronic Excuse-maker

If you hide your sins,
you will not succeed.

Proverbs 28:13 NCV

TODAY'S BIG IDEA!

When things don't go well for you, it's tempting to make excuses. But excuses don't win games and they don't win fans, either. So forget the excuses and think about the next play, not the last one.

What is an excuse? Well, when you make up an excuse, that means that you try to come up with a good reason that you didn't do something that you should have done.

Anybody can make up excuses, and you can too. But you shouldn't get into the habit of making too many excuses. Why? Because excuses don't work in soccer or in life. And why don't they work? Because everybody has already heard so many excuses that almost everybody can recognize excuses when they hear them.

So the next time you're tempted to make up an excuse, don't. Instead of making an excuse, do what you think is right. After all, the very best excuse of all . . . is no excuse.

An excuse is only the skin of
a reason stuffed with a lie.

—

Vance Havner

Making up a string of excuses
is usually harder
than doing the work.

—

Marie T. Freeman

We need to stop focusing on
our lacks and stop giving out
excuses and start looking at
and listening to Jesus.

—

Anne Graham Lotz

Replace your excuses
with fresh determination.

—

Charles Swindoll

DID YOU KNOW?

 In soccer, exhibition games (or teaching scrimmages) are called "friendlies." The meaning of the term is obvious. And, of course, in recreational soccer, all games should be "friendlies."

ONE MORE THING TO REMEMBER

The habit of making excuses is a bad habit. Excuses lead to trouble. If you're in the habit of making excuses, the best day to stop that habit is today.

TODAY'S PRAYER

Dear Lord, when I'm tempted to make excuses, help me be strong as I accept responsibility for my actions.
Amen

CHAPTER 26

Be a Good Loser and a Good Winner

Keep your eyes focused on what is right, and look straight ahead to what is good. Be careful what you do, and always do what is right. Don't turn off the road of goodness; keep away from evil paths.

Proverbs 4:25-27 NCV

TODAY'S BIG IDEA!

Some kids may try to convince you that winning is the most important thing. But the Bible makes it clear that doing what's right is far more important than winning a game.

Okay, since you're a soccer player, it's safe to say that you'd rather play on a winning team. After all, who really likes to lose? Nobody! But here's a question for you to think about: How important is winning? The answer is: It depends.

If you're winning friends for Jesus, or if you're winning against the temptation to do something wrong, then winning is very important. But when it comes to everyday sporting events (like soccer games), winning isn't as important as you might think.

So the next time your team ends up on the losing end of the score, keep things in perspective . . . and don't be too upset. After all, sporting events come and go, and there's always another soccer game to play if you're willing to lace up your cleats. But the really important things in life—like your relationship with God and His Son—last forever. And the eternal victories are the ones that really matter.

Don't let the world define success
for you. Only God can do that.

—

Jim Gallery

Victory is the result of Christ's
life lived out in the believer.
It is important to see that this kind of
victory, not defeat, is God's purpose
for His children.

—

Corrie ten Boom

**We can be victorious,
but only if we walk with God.**

—

Beth Moore

**Never forget: If you belong
to the King, you are on
the winning side.**

—

Billy Graham

DID YOU KNOW?

 In soccer, it's legal to hit the ball with your head, but too much head-hitting may be bad for your health. Some medical studies have found that extensive headers can cause permanent damage. So when it comes to striking the ball with your head, don't overdo it!

ONE MORE THING TO REMEMBER

If you want to be a winner, just try your hardest and be a good sport. When you do, you'll always be a winner, even if your team doesn't score the most goals.

TODAY'S PRAYER

Dear Lord, help me remember that there are many things in life that are more important than winning soccer matches. Help me understand what's really important, Lord, this day and every day.
Amen

CHAPTER 27

No Temper Tantrums

Don't become angry quickly,
because getting angry is foolish.
Ecclesiastes 7:9 NCV

TODAY'S BIG IDEA!

If you lose your cool and throw a temper tantrum, you lose. If you keep your cool and don't throw a tantrum, you win!

Temper tantrums are always silly, whether they happen on the soccer field, at home, or anyplace in between. And pouting is silly. So, of course, is whining. When we lose our tempers, we say things that we shouldn't say, and we do things that we shouldn't do. And it's too bad!

The Bible tells us that it is foolish to become angry and that it is wise to remain calm. That's why we should learn to control our tempers before our tempers control us.

Anger breeds remorse in the heart,
discord in the home,
and bitterness in the community.

—

Billy Graham

Anger is the noise of the soul;
the unseen irritant of the heart.

—

Max Lucado

When you get hot under the collar,
make sure your heart is
prayer-conditioned.

—

Anonymous

If your temper gets the best of you
. . . then other people
get to see the worst in you.

—

Criswell Freeman

DID YOU KNOW?

 For soccer players, the term "tackle" doesn't mean the same thing that it does in American football. In American football, a tackle occurs when one player throws an opposing player to the ground—in soccer, a tackle occurs when one player steals the ball from another player.

NOW HEAR THIS!

In soccer, the greatest barrier to success is the fear of failure.

—

Sven-Göran Eriksson

ONE MORE THING TO REMEMBER

No more tantrums! If you think you're about to pitch a fit or throw a tantrum, slow down, catch your breath, and walk away if you must. It's better to walk away—and keep walking—than it is to blurt out angry words that can't be un-blurted.

TODAY'S PRAYER

Dear Lord, help me to keep away
from angry thoughts and angry
people. And if I am tempted
to have a temper tantrum,
help me to calm down before I do.
Amen

CHAPTER 28

Respecting Authority

The wise are glad to be instructed.

Proverbs 10:8 NLT

TODAY'S BIG IDEA!

Your coach deserves to be treated respect-fully, and so does the referee. And it's up to you to give them the respect they deserve.

Are you polite and respectful to your parents, your teachers, and your coaches? And do you do your best to treat everybody with the respect they deserve? If you want to obey God's rules, then you should be able to answer yes to these questions.

Remember this: the Bible teaches you to be a respectful person—and if it's right there in the Bible, it's certainly the right thing to do!

Great leaders understand that the right attitude will set the right atmosphere, which enables the right response from others.

—

John Maxwell

The next best thing to being wise oneself is to live in a circle of those who are.

—

C. S. Lewis

When God wants to accomplish
something, He calls dedicated men
and women to challenge
His people and lead the way.

—

Warren Wiersbe

The alternative to discipline
is disaster.

—

Vance Havner

DID YOU KNOW?

 In American football, you can't pass the ball to yourself, but in soccer you can! In fact, it's a good way to beat a defender by kicking the ball to an open space on the field and catching up to the ball before the defender does. In fact, this play offers one way to get through the last line of defenders.

ONE MORE THING TO REMEMBER

Everybody is a VIP: VIP means "Very Important Person." To God, everybody is a VIP, and we should treat every person with dignity, patience, and respect.

TODAY'S PRAYER

Dear Lord, give me the maturity
to respect my teachers,
my coaches, and my parents,
today and every day.
Amen

CHAPTER 29

Have Fun!

This is the day the LORD has made.
We will rejoice and be glad in it.
Psalm 118:24 NLT

TODAY'S BIG IDEA!

Games are meant to be fun! So while you're playing soccer, don't forget to enjoy yourself.

The game of soccer is meant to be fun—that's why they call it a game. But sometimes, we take our games a little too seriously. We allow ourselves to become so wrapped up in winning and losing that we forget to have fun. And that's a big mistake!

While you're playing soccer—or doing just about anything else, for that matter—have fun. After all, this is the day the Lord has made, and He wants us to celebrate . . . TODAY!

It is not how much we have,
but how much we enjoy,
that makes our happiness.

—

C. H. Spurgeon

No one is truly happy if he has what
he wants, but only if he wants
something he should have.

—

St. Augustine

**Happiness, like its opposite,
is habit-forming.**

—

Criswell Freeman

**God made round faces;
people make 'em long.**

—

Anonymous

DID YOU KNOW?

⚽ The English term for any type of sports field (including a soccer field) is a "pitch."

⚽ The most common surname of World Cup players is Gonzalez or Gonzales.

⚽ In terms of television audience, it seems that the World Cup easily wins over the Super Bowl. Why? Because while the Super Bowl usually attracts about a hundred million American viewers, it is much less popular in other parts of the world. Meanwhile, the World Cup attracts avid fans from Europe, Asia, South America, and Africa. In fact, it was estimated that 1.1 billion viewers tuned in to the most recent World Cup finals match!

ONE MORE THING TO REMEMBER

The best day to be happy is this one. Don't spend your whole life in the waiting room. Make up your mind to celebrate today.

TODAY'S PRAYER

Dear Lord, You have given me
a priceless gift: the gift of life.
Today I will treasure that
gift and enjoy it.
Amen

CHAPTER 30

Follow Jesus

And whatever you do, in word or in deed, do everything in the name of the Lord Jesus, giving thanks to God the Father through Him.

Colossians 3:17 Holman CSB

TODAY'S BIG IDEA!

Don't take sports too seriously! Whether your team wins or loses isn't really that important. What is important, of course, is that you walk with Jesus every day of your life.

The most important thing you'll ever do in your life has nothing to do with soccer. The most important thing you'll ever do in your life is to make the decision to follow Jesus wherever He leads you.

Jesus wants to have a real relationship with you. Are you willing to have a meaningful relationship with Him? Unless you can answer this question with a great big "Yes," you may miss out on some wonderful things.

This day offers yet another opportunity to behave yourself like a real Christian. When you do, God will guide your steps and bless your life . . . forever.

We have in Jesus Christ
a perfect example of how to put
God's truth into practice.

—

Bill Bright

A believer comes to Christ;
a disciple follows after Him.

—

Vance Havner

Being a Christian is more than just
an instantaneous conversion;
it is like a daily process whereby
you grow to be more
and more like Christ.

—

Billy Graham

Christ is not valued at all unless
He is valued above all.

—

St. Augustine

DID YOU KNOW?

The Manchester United soccer team, which plays in the beloved Old Trafford stadium, is arguably the most popular soccer team in the world. Manchester United is to British soccer what the New York Yankees are to American baseball.

NOW HEAR THIS!

Keep trying to win; keep playing the game; but keep room in your heart for a song.

—

Grantland Rice

ONE MORE THING TO REMEMBER

If you're too afraid of failure, you may not live up to your potential. Remember that failing isn't nearly as bad as failing to try.

TODAY'S PRAYER

Dear Lord, You sent Jesus to save
the world and to save me.
I thank You for Jesus,
and I will do my best to follow Him,
today and forever.
Amen

Bible Verses to
Remember

*For God so loved
the world, that he gave
his only begotten Son,
that whosoever believeth
in him should not perish,
but have everlasting life.*

—

John 3:16 KJV

If someone does wrong to you, do not pay him back by doing wrong to him.

—

Romans 12:17 ICB

*Cast your burden
on the Lord, and He will
support you;
He will never allow
the righteous to be shaken.*

—

Psalm 55:22 Holman CSB

*Do not worry about anything.
But pray and ask God for
everything you need.*

Philippians 4:6 ICB

*Now these three remain:
faith, hope, and love.
But the greatest of these
is love.*

—

1 Corinthians 13:13 Holman CSB

A *friend loves at all times, and a brother is born for a difficult time.*

—

Proverbs 17:17 Holman CSB

I give you a new commandment: that you love one another. Just as I have loved you, you should also love one another.

—

John 13:34 Holman CSB

Finishing is better than starting. Patience is better than pride.

—

Ecclesiastes 7:8 NLT

My Team Photo

My Team

As a way to remember your soccer
teammates, jot down some notes
on the following pages.

Team Name: _Sath's Army_

Year: _2010_

Coach's Name: _Sath_

Phone Number:

E-mail Address:

Something Cool to Remember:

Name: Luke

Position: Forward

Phone Number:

E-mail Address:

Something Cool to Remember: veary good at all posichas

⚽ ⚽ ⚽

Name: Xaviar

Position: Forward

Phone Number:

E-mail Address:

Something Cool to Remember: always tring his to besto

Name: crchanin

Position: Midfelder

Phone Number:

E-mail Address:

Something Cool to Remember: SCORER GOAL

● ● ●

Name: Daniel

Position: Goleie

Phone Number:

E-mail Address:

Something Cool to Remember: Saved almost all the shots in a charmpinship gattie!

Name: Mikey

Position: defender

Phone Number:

E-mail Address:

Something Cool to Remember: let it go... pass e[et] him.

⚽ ⚽ ⚽

Name:

Position:

Phone Number:

E-mail Address:

Something Cool to Remember:

Name:

Position:

Phone Number:

E-mail Address:

Something Cool to Remember:

Name:

Position:

Phone Number:

E-mail Address:

Something Cool to Remember:

Name:

Position:

Phone Number:

E-mail Address:

Something Cool to Remember:

Name:

Position:

Phone Number:

E-mail Address:

Something Cool to Remember:

Name:

Position:

Phone Number:

E-mail Address:

Something Cool to Remember:

🐾 🐾 🐾

Name:

Position:

Phone Number:

E-mail Address:

Something Cool to Remember:

Name:

Position:

Phone Number:

E-mail Address:

Something Cool to Remember:

Name:

Position:

Phone Number:

E-mail Address:

Something Cool to Remember:

Name:

Position:

Phone Number:

E-mail Address:

Something Cool to Remember:

Name:

Position:

Phone Number:

E-mail Address:

Something Cool to Remember:

For when the one Great Scorer
comes to write against
your name, He marks not
that you won or lost,
but how you played the game.

—

Grantland Rice